Colores: rojo
Colors: Red

Esther Sarfatti

Rourke
Publishing LLC
Vero Beach, Florida 32964

www.rourkepublishing.com

PHOTO CREDITS: © Glenda Powers: title page; © Viorika Prikhodko: page 3; © Studio One: page 5; © Andrey Beka: page 7; © Russell McCollom: page 11; © Varina and Jay Patel: page 15; © Mark Evans: page 21; © Matej Michelizza, Jan Rihak, Jeremy Edwards: page 23.

Editor: Robert Stengard-Olliges

Cover design by Nicola Stratford, bdpublishing.com

Library of Congress Cataloging-in-Publication Data

Sarfatti, Esther.
 Colors : red / Esther Sarfatti.
   p. cm. -- (Concepts)
 ISBN 978-1-60044-519-4 (Hardcover)
 ISBN 978-1-60044-660-3 (Softcover)
 1. Colors--Juvenile literature. 2. Red--Juvenile literature. I. Title.
  QC495.5.S357 2008
  535.6--dc22
                          2007014031

Printed in the USA

CG/CG

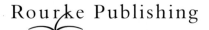

Rourke Publishing

www.rourkepublishing.com – rourke@rourkepublishing.com
Post Office Box 3328, Vero Beach, FL 32964

Esta página es roja.
This page is red.

El rojo es mi color favorito.

Red is my favorite color.

Me gustan las
manzanas rojas.

I like red apples.

Me gustan los creyones rojos.

I like red crayons.

Me gustan los camiones de bomberos rojos.

I like red fire engines.

11

Me gustan mis botas rojas.

I like my red boots.

Me gusta mi traje de baño rojo.

I like my red bathing suit.

15

Me gustan las
mariquitas rojas.

I like red ladybugs.

Me gustan las cerezas rojas.

I like red cherries.

Me gustan los autos de carreras rojos.

I like red race cars.

Hay muchas cosas rojas.
¿Te gusta el rojo también?

So many things are red.
Do you like red, too?

23

Índice

Index

botas   12
crayones   8
manzanas   6
mariquitas   16

apples   6
boots   12
crayons   8
ladybugs   16

Lecturas adicionales / Further Reading

Anderson, Moira. Finding Colors: *Red*. Heinemann, 2005.

Schuette, Sarah L. *Red: Seeing Red All Around Us*. Capstone Press, 2006.

Páginas Web recomendadas / Recommended Websites

www.enchantedlearning.com/colors/red.shtml

Acerca de la autora / About the Author

Esther Sarfatti lleva más de 15 años trabajando con libros infantiles como editora y traductora. Ésta es su primera serie como autora. Nacida en Brooklyn, Nueva York, donde creció en una familia trilingüe, Esther vive actualmente en Madrid, España, con su esposo y su hijo.

Esther Sarfatti has worked with children's books for over 15 years as an editor and translator. This is her first series as an author. Born in Brooklyn, New York, and brought up in a trilingual home, Esther currently lives with her husband and son in Madrid, Spain.